MED LABANE

Morocco:

MED LABANE

Morocco:

Joys and sorrows of a determined nation.

JustFiction Edition

Imprint

Cover image: www.ingimage.com

Publisher:
JustFiction! Edition
is a trademark of
Dodo Books Indian Ocean Ltd. and OmniScriptum S.R.L publishing group

120 High Road, East Finchley, London, N2 9ED, United Kingdom
Str. Armeneasca 28/1, office 1, Chisinau MD-2012, Republic of Moldova, Europe
Printed at: see last page
ISBN: 978-620-6-74218-0

Morocco:

Joys and sorrows of a determined nation.

Medlabane.auteur@gmail.com

MED LABANE

Morocco:

Joys and sorrows of a determined nation

Local novel.

Contents.

Chapter1
Morocco through the ages.

"Cradle of free men, source of enlightenment.
Land of sovereignty and land of peace.
May sovereignty and peace be forever united.
You lived among nations, like a sublime title.
Filling every heart, declaimed by every tongue.
By soul, by body, your champion has risen, and answered your call.
And in my mouth, and in my blood, your love shook light and embers.
My brothers, let's go to the highest.
We'll proclaim to the world that this is where we live.With God, the Fatherland, the King as our standard".

National anthem of Morocco.

The national anthem, imbued with the spirit of citizenship, is rooted in the hearts of Moroccans the world over. A standard that remains a precious weapon for a people ready to perish in order to cherish it forever, it is their pride rooted in the depths of their soul, whether Arab, Berber, Sahrawi, Jewish, Christian or Muslim.

Morocco, the land of the setting sun, has long been a land of welcome par excellence. With its flag standing majestically on an impassable red carpet, adorned with a green-colored star of peace and coexistence, it floats like a tree whose roots are planted in Africa and branches extend towards Europe. Let's discover its ancestral history, offering an admirably rich foliage.

Morocco, with its official language emanating from its Holy Book and its religious teachings, as well as its strong family cohesion, in addition to its dependence on agriculture as a basic resource, is very much like a local novel driven by fundamental values to remain forever great.

According to the latest census, Morocco's current population is 36.67 million. 50.2% of whom are women, 64.3% urban dwellers, 56.6% of working age, 25.2% children and 12.2% elderly.

But Morocco's identity began a long time ago. This country at the crossroads of the worlds is a veritable treasure trove of history and culture, silently witnessing the rise and fall of major civilizations since the dawn of time. In this story, we discover some of the influences that have forged its particularity, and follow the archaeological traces indicating human presence from prehistoric times.

- The world is Moroccan: the first inhabitants, hunter-gatherers, left traces of their existence in the caves and rock shelters scattered across its regions. Before the arrival of the great civilizations, these ancestors created the Moroccan landscape some 315,000 years ago, confirming that the oldest known representative of our species, Homo sapiens, lived in Morocco*.

Tafouralt Pigeons cave.

The first surgeon and patient to be operated on also lived there, and the world's first surgical operation, known as "Trepanation" **, was performed in a cave in the northeast of the country, nicknamed "Tafouralt Pigeons cave".

According to *Abbe Jean Roche*, a French prehistorian specializing in the Upper Palaeolithic of Morocco and Portugal (1913-2008), the Pigeon cave also functioned as a necropolis during the Upper Palaeolithic period. Excavations by *Abbe Jean Roche* unearthed more than 180 skeletons, which have been the subject of a fascinating detailed study by French archaeologist *Denise Ferembach*. A skeleton was also exhumed from the necropolis level, its skull showing traces of trepanning considered to be the oldest in the world. X-rays showed a pre-existing healing process, implying that the individual had survived the operation***. The archaeologists trace their research back to the archaeological level in which the skull was discovered, to a date between 11,000 and 12,000 years ago, making the trepanned skull the first operated on in human history.

*****

*The discovery, made by an international team led by (*Jean-Jacques Hublin*: Max-Planck Institute for Evolutionary Anthropology in Leipzig and College de France). Le Monde newspaper 07 June 2017 by *Hervé Morin*.

**Trepanation: surgical operation consisting in cutting a hole in a bone. Brain tumor in particular.

*** Wikipedia source: Tafouralt Pigeons cave.

Ancient Morocco was home to a variety of different cultures and influences. The Phoenicians, who were great navigators, founded colonies on the country's coasts, contributing to the growth of trade in the region.

In the 1st century BC, the Romans conquered part of the territory and brought with them their architecture, language and way of life. The ruins of Volubilis, near the city of Meknes, bear witness to this.

Volubilis, ancient Roman city.

At that time, Morocco had relations with Carthaginian society, which was known for its maritime explorations and impact on the western Mediterranean region. Moroccan heritage was profoundly influenced by these cultural exchanges.

The emergence of Islam in the 7th century is one of the most important moments in Morocco's history. The region was conquered by Muslims under the rule of the Umayyads and became a center of the Islamic faith. Fez, the country's cultural capital, has been an intellectual hub ever since, attracting scientists and scholars from all over the Muslim world to its "Al Quaraouiyine" university. The latter is considered the world's first university, founded under the Idrissids in 859 by a pious and wealthy Moroccan woman who used her fortune to establish this educational institution. *Fatima Fihria*'s legacy lives on in this building, which has played a major role in the history of education and Islamic culture. We're still in the 9th century, when the role of Moroccan women was already shining brightly.

Statue of Fatima Fihria at the Jordan Museum in Amman.

The Moroccan landscape has been permanently marked by Islamic architecture, characterized by its magnificent mosques and mosaic-adorned palaces. A remarkable example of this architectural heritage is the medina of Fez or Marrakech, with its quarters and lively souks.

- The great imperial dynasties of Moroccan history:

The Idrisside Dynasty (789-974): Founded by *Idriss I*, this is considered the first to rule Morocco. It established its capital in Fez and played a major role in the Islamization of the region.

The Almoravid Dynasty (1060-1147): The Almoravids built a powerful empire in the 11th century under the reign of *Youssouf Ibnou Tachfine*. They originated from the Sahara region and unified the Morocco and much of Muslim Spain, leading to a period of cultural and economic wealth.

The Almohad Dynasty (1147-1269): The Almohads succeeded the Almoravids and continued the expansion of the Muslim empire in Spain and the Maghreb. They built famous monuments such as the Koutoubia mosque in Marrakech. This dynasty had a significant impact on the country's history.

The Marinid Dynasty (1244-1465): The Marinids overthrew the Almohads and established their own reign, centered mainly on Fez. They played an important role in the fight against the Crusades in North Africa.

The Saadian Dynasty (1554-1659): The Saadians emerged at the end of the 16th century and established their power in Marrakech. They contributed to the territorial expansion of Morocco, which reached the apogee of its civilization under the reign of Sultan *Ahmed Al Mansour Ad-dahbi*: Ahmed the Golden Victorious.

The Alaouite Dynasty (since 1666) : The Cherifian Kingdom's actual dynasty was founded by *Moulay Rachid*, and his descendants have ruled the country from the 17th century to the present day, with King *Mohammed VI* currently in power.

These dynasties have had a significant impact on the country's history, playing an essential role in the development of its culture and politics over the centuries, helping to shape it as it is today.

During the 19th century, Morocco was the scene of a conflict between the Euro-Mediterranean colonial powers. France and Spain colonized it and left deep scars on Moroccan society.

Its politics, economy and culture were affected by foreign occupation. Sultan *Mohammed V* led the Moroccan nationalist movement that worked to gain the country's independence.

Morocco finally became sovereign in 1956, ending decades of colonization.

- Morocco's cultural wealth:

Moroccan culture is made up of a variety of practices, traditions and influences. It is present in all aspects of daily life, from cuisine to music and crafts. Moroccan gastronomy is famous for its refinement and variety, which makes it attractive the world over. Moroccan dishes are a veritable symphony of spice and aroma, with ingredients such as cumin, coriander, cinnamon and saffron adding a unique depth of flavor.

Moroccan cuisine is characterized by the tajine, a simmered dish prepared in a terracotta vessel of the same name. Restaurants feature a variety of tagines, from lamb with prunes and almonds to chicken confit with olives.

Moroccan handicrafts: the colorful tagine.

The bustling markets, also known as souks, showcase fresh produce, multi-colored spices and local crafts. They offer an unforgettable sensory experience where visitors can discover street food and taste the delights of Moroccan gastronomy. From mechoui to couscous, ending the feast with mint tea accompanied by delicious pastries such as gazelle horns, the appetite is simply delighted. A visit to Marrakech's famous Jamâa el Fna square is definitely worth the detour.

The music of Morocco is an assortment of styles and influences. It combines the rhythms of classical Arabic, Arabo-Andalusian, Judeo-Christian, Berber and African music. The oud, a plucked lute that creates enchanting melodies, is one of the most famous instruments.

Gnawa, or Moroccan jazz, is a mystical musical form derived from African customs, distinguished by its hypnotic rhythm and its traditional instrument, the guembri. The annual Gnawa music festival in Essaouira (formerly Mogador) and the Andalusian music and Sufi chant festival in Fez reflect the nation's cultural diversity and testify to its rich historical past.

Travelling back in time to Morocco through the ages, with its diverse culture, is a tangible testimony to this complex history. The country has gone through tumultuous times to become the jewel it is today, from the first prehistoric inhabitants to the imperial dynasties, via the period of colonization and the struggle for independence.

Morocco's resources come mainly from phosphate (leading producer), agriculture, fishing and tourism. It does not rank among the industrialized countries with significant economic reserves of oil and gas. However, thanks to its human resources, political stability and wise diplomacy, which distinguish it from the rest of the countries in its region, as well as its geographical location and strategic view of two seas and continents, it has become a continental leader and an enviable model for development and investment.

When the Lions roar.

Chapter 2
Joy.

December 2022:

"Of your lands, your waters, your mountains.
Of your air, your cities and countryside.
From all your trees and all the stones that litter your soil, O Morocco!
The home of free men, the radiance of enlightenment.
The forum of peace and protection.
The kiss of lovers and the home of the generous and honorable.
The Morocco of glories among nations.
The homeland of Arabs, Berbers and the Sahara.
From which the armies of conquest set out to build their civilization on the land of Andalusia.
In which lie the majestic Atlas Mountains, home to lions".

Khalil Al Boulouchi. Translated poem.

Journalist *Khalil Al Boulouchi.*

This is how the famous Omani sports commentator *Khalil Al Boulouchi* opened his comments on the Moroccan national team's matches during the Qatar World Cup. His powerful, enthusiastic expressions moved fans across the Arab world and set the hearts of television viewers aflame.

Morocco's achievement in the World Cup has had a significant impact and generated great pride throughout the Arab world, Africa, as well as in some Latin American and Asian countries. This sporting success transcends national and cultural boundaries. Support for Morocco comes in part from the Arab world, which sees the Moroccan performance as a source of inspiration for its entire community, demonstrating that perseverance and talent can lead to international recognition. For Africa, this success is a source of continental pride and reinforces the idea that African teams can compete at the highest level of world soccer.

Support from countries in Asia and Latin America has also shown admiration for Morocco's progress in the competition.

Overall, this support and pride stems from a belief in the ability of emerging nations to shine on the international stage, whether in sport, culture or other fields, showing that a country's success can inspire and serve as a model uniting communities around the world.

Morocco's desire to take part in the World Cup is an epic that crosses soccer stadiums and penetrates the minds and hearts of an entire people. It is the story of its national soccer team and the all-consuming passion of its fans, a story based on high points, sacrifices and the unity of an entire nation.

While many national teams want to take part in the World Cup, Morocco is far happier to do so. The country has embarked on this challenge with unshakeable determination.

The road to qualification in Qatar is a difficult one. The "Atlas Lions" are determined to do whatever it takes to succeed. The players have come together to achieve a single goal: to display their country and its pride on an international scale.

The national team reflects diversity, with players from predominantly European countries united by a common passion: a deep love for their homeland.

Laughter after qualifying for the quarterfinals.

The players carry the weight of an entire country on their shoulders, as well as that of their coach, nicknamed "avocado head", and they do so with "niyya", which means good intention. An expression coined by coach *Walid Regragui* at a press conference, out of either wisdom or irritation. This latter has since become the fruit that sows Baraka and nurtures confidence in day-to-day relations.

Morocco stands out for its exemplary work in sports facilities, setting up world-renowned training centers and academies. These facilities are equipped with state-of-the-art technology and infrastructure, rivalling the best in the world. This dedication is reflected in the total commitment of all hierarchies and personnel involved, from coaches to administrators, to persevere and take the country to the highest level in various sporting disciplines. Morocco has shown its determination to train and develop local talent, creating a pool of world-class athletes ready to proudly represent the country on the international stage.

When passion crosses borders:

The Atlas Lions are not the only ones to embark on this adventure. Every time they meet, a 12th player who is responsible for keeping an eye on them accompanies them. Soccer fans are not only spectators; they also play a driving role and provide real moral support for the team

Red frenzy during the national anthem.

What was particularly surprising in Qatar was the turnout of men, women and children from all over the world to support the Moroccan team, far exceeding expectations in terms of national representation. So impressive was a mobilization that virtually no other team could match it in terms of support. The "twelfth player," as he is often called, was a real force, creating a nightmare for opposing teams. At times, their passionate support seemed to outweigh the efforts of the eleven players on the pitch, demonstrating the power of unity and enthusiasm that can transcend the confines of the playing field.

Famous for their unprecedented fervor, they gather in stadiums, dressed in red and green, waving their flags and chanting in support. The atmosphere is electrified by an energy that turns the stands into a sea of red. When the Moroccan national anthem is sung in the stadium, it's a sacred occasion of togetherness, with thousands of people rising in chorus to sing with pride.

Every moment of the match is lived and enjoyed by the fans, who share their emotion, tension and ecstasy with their team. Moroccans' affection for their national team extends beyond the stadiums. It expands into the streets, cafes, town halls and even workplaces. The streets are filled with people who gather to watch the matches on large screens set up in public squares. Families come together in front of their TVs, while children in rural areas are ecstatic in front of small screens or battery-operated radios, recalling the atmosphere of the famous Moroccan radio series "Al Azalia", broadcast in the good old days of the seventies on the national radio.

The series, named "the eternal", was very popular with Moroccans. Generations still remember how this radio drama created events, given the suspense that characterized its episodes. It was comparable to the iconic 1960s British series "Doctor Who", which acquired legendary status in the world of science fiction. The series features the Doctor, a Time Lord traveling through time and space in a spaceship called the TARDIS. Famous for its blend of science fiction, adventure and exploration of temporal concepts, it has exerted a profound influence on British culture and television in general.

The team's performance, their game strategy and the hope of qualification were inescapable topics of daily discussion. Soccer becomes a source of collective pride and joy that transcends social boundaries, uniting people from all occupations around a common interest. During the qualification phases, the Moroccan national team wins unprecedented events. Streets all over the country are transformed into one big party with jubilant crowds. Horns honked, flags waved and people danced to the rhythm of the youyous. The joy and pride of an entire people did not deter His Majesty, the supreme leader, from taking to the streets to share the same euphoria with his people.

King Mohamed VI in the streets of Rabat after qualifying for the quarterfinals.

The Moroccan national team's journey to Qatar was marked by many sacrifices, efforts and moments of success. However, the fans were behind them every step of the way, with a remarkable passion to support them.

The Atlas Lions in Qatar were more than just a soccer team, they were, and still are, a dream for a nation united behind them. Whatever the result, this team and its journey will be etched in Morocco's history forever, as a shining testament to strength, determination and unity.

Whatever the outcome, Morocco will keep its share of pride, rewarded by the tremendous work of the artisan in charge of making the World Cup at the Italian company "GDF Bertoni"; renowned for its trophies and medals, and who is unquestionably Moroccan *Ahmed Ait Sidi Ab-delkader.*

Ahmed Ait Sidi Abdelkader: History of a world trophy.

The fervor of the fans extends far beyond the country's borders. Millions of Moroccans gather in Diasporas around the world to support their team, strengthening the bond with their compatriots and reinforcing their national identity. In many cities, they came together to demonstrate a spirit of camaraderie and enthusiasm.They organized parades, proudly displaying their flags, wearing their team jerseys and sharing photos and videos on the networks. Prayers and blessings were heard everywhere, from pubs in New York to public squares in Paris, in Gaza and Tel Aviv. Fan fervor transcends geographical and religious boundaries, uniting an entire nation behind its national anthem"God, the Fatherland, the King".

Joy transcends borders.

Times of celebration are particularly festive. When a player scores a goal, he goes to his mother to embrace her, seeking her blessing. Then he prostrates himself face down on the ground, praising Allah, ready to be carried away by his fans in a wave of affection and gratitude. These latters celebrate the triumph, cover him with flags and express their love for him with inexpressible emotion.

Achraf Hakimi and Sofiane Boufal. Joy with Mum.

Beyond the fervor for soccer, the journey of the team embodies a sacred alliance. Moroccans from all regions, social strata, and generations unite behind a common purpose: their nation's triumph on the global stage.

During the qualifying matches, regional rivalries fade, political differences diminish and the country coalesces as one cohesive family. It's a time of transcendence, when the primacy of national identity supersedes all other considerations. The evidence lies in the photo of *Lino Bacco**, which stirred an entire nation and signifies an unwavering allegiance to a nation that recognizes no distinctions among its citizens based on their origins or beliefs.

Throughout this period, many, whether Moroccan citizens or simply sympathizers, came together in celebration to support the national team, exuberantly chanting cries of 'Sir, Sir,' signifying encouragement, akin to the British YouTuber *Thogden.*

Lino Bacco's precious tears. *The Broroccan Thogden.*

**Lino Bacco*, whose birth name is *Louis Gaspard Lobianco*, is an Italian sports journalist born in Casablanca, where his family has been rooted for over a century.

Two of the most famous players in this category are *Achraf Hakimi* and *Hakim Ziyech*. The former began his professional career with Real Madrid. He later moved to Borussia Dortmund, Inter Milan and recently Paris Saint-Germain. The second excelled with Ajax Amsterdam before re-joining Chelsea. Both bi-nationals have preferred the red and green colors and have achieved great success with the national team, helping the Atlas Lions to reach the semi-finals of the World Cup. Their fans admire them for their talent and dedication to their country.

Hakim Zyech and Achraf Hakimi after the match against Spain.

This compelling story of the national team and its dedicated fans is a testament to the strength of a people to break the glass ceiling, overcome challenges and lift their country. It's a celebration of the passion, pride and unity that make up a community ready to support their team to the end, and to accompany them to the gates of the royal palace in Rabat, where the nation's spiritual father awaited them in turn with a warm welcome.

The warm welcome reserved for the Atlas Lions by His Majesty the King and his people

July 8, 2023: a new feat in golden ink.

The U23 national team's victory in the continental championship consolidated the phenomenal work of the players and the Royal Federation. A feat that testifies to the determination of an entire country to raise its flag to the highest level. Morocco has thus won its first African title for this age group, and the adventure continues for these champions, who look forward to meeting us in Paris for the next Olympic Games in 2024.

Morocco 2023 African champion.

July 20, 2023: Women's World Cup Australia and New Zealand.

This time, it's the Atlas Lionesses' turn to prove their determination and make history. Their mission will be to consolidate their role in the ceremonial register and promote their homeland in this international forum.

Therefore, it shall be. The women's team achieved an exceptional feat under the guidance of Frensh Coach *Reynald Pedros*. His tears of joy after qualifying for the second round, and his singing of the national anthem at the start of the matches, moved a whole nation. "Allah, Al Watan, Al Malik".

The women's national team made history just like their male counterparts, reaching the Round of 16 in their very first appearance at the World Cup, something no other Arab country has been able to achieve.

The Atlas Lionesses qualify for the second round.

- The Moroccan diaspora:

Although Moroccans come from a variety of ethnic and religious backgrounds, their attachment to their country remains a sacred symbol.

The Moroccan diaspora remains a crucial driving force, serving as a bridge between their homeland and their country of residence.

Whether Jewish, Christian or Muslim, but above all Moroccan, these representatives are the ambassadors of parallel diplomacy.

As the list is long, only a few names representing Morocco on the international stage will be mentioned, without forgetting the importance of the contribution of all the other personalities.

Serge Berdugo: Former Minister. President of the Rassemblement mondial du Judaïsme marocain and leader of the Moroccan Jewish community.

Rachid Yazami: Moroccan physical chemist and inventor of the graphite anode for lithium-ion batteries.

Richard Attias: Moroccan businessperson and international communicator. Alongside Éric Zemmour, he declared in an interview with a France 5 journalist:

- *Richard Attias*! Do you feel patriotic?

- Yes, I am very attached to my country, Morocco. I really have deep roots in my country. When the Vichy regime arrived in Morocco, and the late King *Mohamed V* was asked to give up the Jews, he replied:

"If you want to take them, you take me first". So I think it's this duty to memory that keeps me Moroccan.

Rajaa Cherkaoui El Moursli: researcher specializing in nuclear physics. L'Oréal-Unesco Prize for Women in Science in 2015.

Marc Lasry, nicknamed "The Moroccan Freak", is an influential media figure in the United States. Director of one of the world's most successful investment funds and owner of the legendary Milwaukee NBA club.

Gad El Maleh: Actor, comedian, director.

Jamal Debbouze: Actor, comedian.

Nawal Moutawakkil: International athlete, gold medallist in the first women's 400m hurdles in the history of the 1984 Los Angeles Olympic Games.

Yariv El Baz: Businessman described by the New York Times as one of the intermediaries in the deal between the USA and Morocco.

Moncef Slaoui: Biological researcher appointed by *Donald Trump* in 2020 to head the "Warp Speed" operation to manufacture the anti-Covid vaccine.

Asmaa Boujibar: First Moroccan woman to join NASA. Geophysicist, research professor at Western Washington University.

Kamal El Oudghiri: NASA space engineer.

Samir Machhour: Vice-president of Samsung biolo-gics.

Yossi Dahan: Founder of the Eldan Group. The Israeli businessperson of Moroccan origin who has promised a huge bonus to the Atlas Lions during the world cup 2022. In an interview reported by the Israeli Jewish news website lphinfo.com, he said the day after Morocco is qualifying for the quarterfinals: "I don't think there's a word in Hebrew to express my joy. I'm out of Morocco, but Morocco is still in me".

Abdeljabbar El Manira: Professor of neuroscience, elected member of the Royal Swedish Academy of Sciences in 2015, first Arab researcher member of the Nobel Prize in Medicine jury.

Faouzi Annajah: Engineer, founder of NAMX: First hydrogen vehicle "made in Morocco".

Michel Ohayon: Businessman and owner of several hotels around the world, including the Waldorf Astoria in Jerusalem, the Grand Hotel in Bordeaux, and some twenty Galeries Lafayette stores.

Your compatriots bow to you with respect "Ladies and Gentlemen".

The banner "God, the fatherland, the King" lights up Agadir.

Many thanks to you all.

The years 2022 and 2023 were marked by joy and passion thanks to the exploits of the lions and lionesses, whether at continental or world level.

Nevertheless, the year 2023 is not yet over, and Moroccans will face a new, tough test this time, which will cost the lives of thousands of their compatriots.

"We are from you and for you".

The Atlas Lions donate all their bonuses to the earthquake victims, until the CAN 2024 in Ivory Coast. LE MATIN newspaper, September 12, 2023.

Chapter 3
The challenge.

"When the earth is shaken by its tremor. When the earth throws off its burdens. When man asks, what is happening to it? On that day, she will tell her own story, according to what her Lord has revealed to her." *Holy Koran, 99: The Shaking.*

- United for reconstruction.

On Friday, September 8, 2023, Marrakech shines brightly before tragedy strikes the region. At 11:11pm local time, a 7° magnitude earthquake struck southern Morocco.

As on all other days, Marrakech began its daytime with the streets bustling with activity, the tourists at the rendezvous. Then, on that fateful night, as the inhabitants of the Al-Haouz province slept - their final sleep for thousands of people - the earth shook and the whole region, deep in the rocky mountains, felt a dull roar followed by devastating aftershocks, knocking down centuries old houses in clouds of dust, trapping people under rubble, causing loss of life and spreading panic.

As ambulance sirens echoed through the streets and rescue teams rushed to the scene, the human soul did not waver. In the midst of the ruins, a glimmer of hope sprang up, galvanizing the capacity and resilience of the people. Moroccans immediately mobilized and demonstrated exceptional solidarity.

As the first witnesses to the disaster rushed to help, the fans who had supported their national team all the way to Qatar during the World Cup festivities began to gather en masse to support their survivors this time, and to accompany their deceased to their last demeasure.

With great determination, rescue teams, firefighters, paramedics, volunteers and police forces mobilized. They braved the unstable rubble to extract survivors, provide emergency medical care and comfort traumatized people. The civic mindedness and determination of an entire people to get back on their feet immediately was demonstrated by the countless queues for blood donations, the invasion of supermarkets to buy all the necessary provisions, and the tide of convoys from all over the kingdom. Their dedication, as well as their moral and material support, raised more than a few questions about the creativity of this amazing people.

Solidarity Morocco: blood donations, convoys, food. Ready to do anything for our children; tomorrow's generation.

Therefore, the protagonists of the tragedy are not only the rescue professionals. Ordinary people, anonymous heroes, performed acts of bravery on the scene. Residents supported their neighbors, strangers came together to help, and vendors opened their shops to offer shelter and food.

Omar, manager of a restaurant on the road between Marrakech and Taroudant, explained to journalist how remarkable the solidarity had been, as hundreds of convoys loaded to the brim passed by. Since the beginning of the humanitarian actions, he has mobilized his team to provide free meals to volunteer travelers.

As a shopkeeper, he declares, "I witnessed the distress caused by the earthquake. I immediately felt the need to help in any way I could, then i decided to open the doors of my restaurant to welcome volunteers. It was incredible to see the extent to which people rallied to lend their support. I did my best, offering free board and lodging to the couriers so they could rest and recharge their batteries.

It was a moving and gratifying experience to see our community come together in a time of crisis. I'm proud to have been able to contribute to this collective effort.

Rachid, owner of an inn along the picturesque Tizin Tichka road, became an unforgettable figure for volunteers traveling to the scene of the disaster. His selfless support and generous gestures left a lasting impression. Like *Omar*, he opened his doors, offering a place to rest and recuperate. His support was not limited to hospitality; he also provided meals and drinks, ensuring that volunteers were well fed and hydrated. His commitment to their well-being was evident, and his hostel quickly became a rallying point for those who were devoting their efforts to helping the victims. His example showed how one person and one place can become a beacon of hope and humanity in the midst of adversity.

The extent of the damage, a village in ruins.

In the midst of the tragedy, King *Mohamed VI* sent a powerful message to the nation by committing himself to blood donation. Unlike Western messages broadcast on TV, His Majesty's message was delivered from the heart - the heart of a monarch, but above all, of a father who knows how to communicate with his children through deeds. The Moroccans are well aware of this language, which solemnly calls for the unity that is so deeply rooted in their customs.

His visit to the hospitals to comfort the survivors was an interpretation of the role expected of a people united to face this difficult period. His strength in overcoming this catastrophe will be his cohesion, his solidarity and his ability to resist. Throughout the country, the King's compassion has inspired a sense of unity and determination. Moroccans realize that rebuilding will involve not only material work, but also spirituality. This is an opportunity to demonstrate to the world the strength of this people, their ability to stand up and support each other.

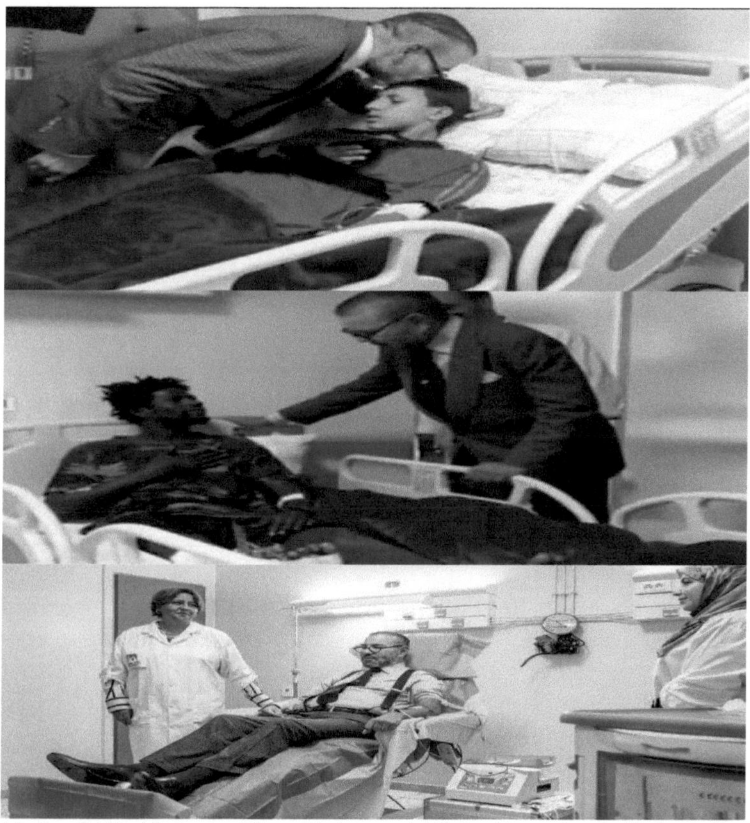

Visit of His Majesty King Mohamed VI to Marrakech University Hospital on September 12, 2023.

The King has urgently set up a fund to collect the funds needed to rebuild the affected areas. Morocco will rebuild its remote regions with a new architecture that will probably preserve the traditional aspect, but will certainly adapt to safety standards.

September 14, 2023 at the Royal Palace in Rabat, a working meeting chaired by King Mohamed VI, devoted to the emergency program to care for the victims of the Al-Haouz earthquake.

The earthquake, which shook six of the Kingdom's regions - Marrakech, Al-Haouz, Chichaoua, Taroudant, Ouarzazate and Azilal -, left a deep imprint on these southern provinces. No fewer than 163 towns were hard-hit by the disaster, affecting a population of 2.8 million. A total of 2,930 rural areas and douars were affected, while the number of buildings destroyed totalled 5, 9674.

Morocco's rapid response to this tragedy was exemplary. His Majesty chaired an exceptional working meeting, during which he issued priority directives to all institutions to immediately initiate relief operations for the victims. On the ground, he also ordered the creation of a special account to manage the consequences of the earthquake. This financial support is intended to provide direct assistance to affected families who have lost all or part of their homes. In addition, it launched a program for the reconstruction and rehabilitation of devastated areas, based on a well thought out, integrated and ambitious approach.

This program includes restoring affected buildings, reinforcing infrastructure and improving the quality of public services, with the aim of restoring normal life to these hard-hit regions.

The imperative duty of government institutions is now to give far greater priority to these vulnerable regions. Yet, in the face of these seismic disasters, many questions are being asked at the same time about the risks surrounding the country. However, before delving into this subject, it is essential to adopt a precise scientific perspective on the situation, and recognize that its geographical location makes it inevitably exposed on an ongoing basis.

Throughout the various periods of its history, Morocco has been exposed to a series of earthquakes, varying in severity, due to its geographical position at the heart of a convergent zone between two major tectonic plates, African and Eurasian, which profoundly affects it and makes it vulnerable to the vibrations resulting from the collision of these two moving masses.

In May 1078, an earthquake shook the shores of Gibraltar, followed on December 31, 1079 by another that struck the city of Larache, resulting in the loss of many human lives. The city of Fez also witnessed several earthquakes in 1522, 1624, 1755 and 1773. The 1624 earthquake was particularly destructive, affecting the towns of Taza, Fez and Meknes. On August 5, 1660, Melilla was on the brink of a major seismic catastrophe, causing loss of life and enormous material damage. In 1719, the country was hit on the Atlantic coast, reaching as far as Marrakech, where it caused extensive material damage.

However, the most powerful earthquake of recent decades was the one that devastated Agadir in 1960, reaching a magnitude of 5.7 on the Richter scale and almost completely destroying the town. Sadly, the disaster claimed the lives of nearly 15,000 people, around two-thirds of the city's population at the time. The need to rebuild the city in its entirety was imperative. Subsequently, the Al Hoceima earthquake in 1994 left deep scars, followed by another one on February 24, 2004, with a magnitude of 6°, which unfortunately caused the death of 600 people and hundreds of injuries.

Seismic tremors have been a constant throughout its past and the country is fully aware - and I would like to stress once again the importance of this scientific perspective - that future earthquakes cannot be ruled out, as long as our universe endures. The kingdom is aware of this, but convinced that hazards will never weaken it, knowing that whatever cannot kill Simba completely will make him even stronger.

The national team, which had been supported a few months earlier by today's deceased, is in turn involved in this mission, giving its blood and promising its commitment to other equally important actions for reconstruction.

Times change, one day for and one day against. In this crisis, it was the national team's duty to play its part as citizens and support its supporters in their ordeal. O how many of those injured in the tragedy were ready to give their blood a few months earlier to help their little thumb grow up, win the world trophy and take it home with them. Today, they are rescued with the blood of their King, their compatriots and their beloved team.

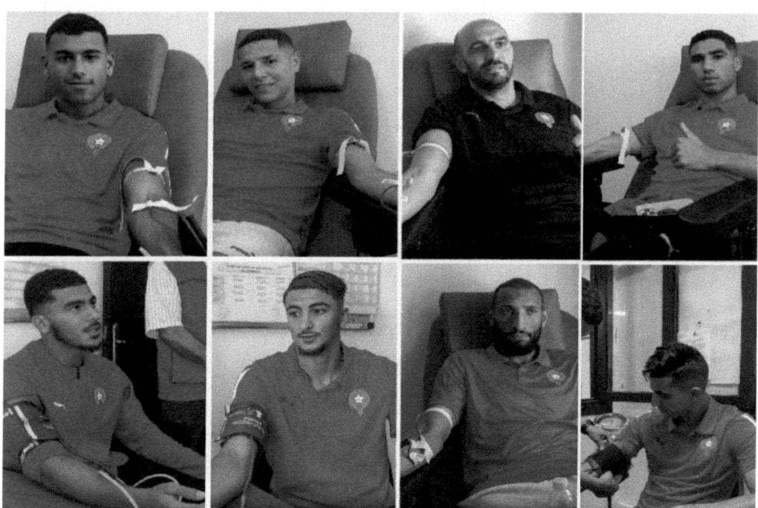

Atlas Lions, it's your turn to show solidarity.

The Al-Haouz region is beginning to rise from the ashes, and hope is gradually covering the dark days. Several Moroccan and foreign associations and charitable organizations have taken part in the humanitarian action, led by volunteers who have joined the rescue teams in a spirit of solidarity to help the victims.

Although physical reconstruction is a considerable challenge, it is sustained by hope and perseverance. The resilience of an entire people will enable Marrakech and its region to rise stronger than ever.

A street in Marrakech's medina affected by the earthquake.

When we look back, we can see just how capable humanity is in the face of adversity. The acts of bravery, generosity and solidarity that resulted from this ordeal can inspire us. This tragedy is an example of how a nation can come together, united and determined to create a bright future.

In Marrakech, the scars are deeper than ever, leaving an indelible mark of the most severe ordeal the thousand-year-old city has ever known. Whether hidden beneath layers of dusty memory or etched in mountainous stone, the after-effects of the past will remain silent witnesses to history.

When the earth moved, I went out into the street like all the people of Casablanca for fear of a possible collapse. Before the tremor, there was a huge noise, as if a train was passing overhead. Despite the solidity of the building in which i live and its compliance with safety standards, the akathisia of the earth was felt so strongly that the tremor was strong. My family and i left the apartment to take shelter in a public space, where we spent a few hours hoping there would be no further aftershocks. At the time, I had no idea that the whole Marrakech region was suffering more, and the shock was only more frightening the following morning when we learned of the scale of the earthquake, which had devastated entire villages, causing considerable material and human damage. The images of the first moments after the earthquake were striking. Entire villages had been turned into ruins, and historical buildings and minarets, which had once stood proudly in the sky, had turned into heaps of stone and dust.

An earthquake that caused unprecedented damage hit the region, but it also demonstrated the resilience of an entire people, which is profounded in their spirit.

A mourning population, a long night in Jamâa El Fna square.

The cries of despair and pain were heartbreaking, as support teams struggled to repair the damage in a relentless search for survivors. Families were torn apart, lives were lost and a region full of life sank into mourning.

However, in this period of terror, a glimmer of hope appeared thanks to the great cohesion of the population, which subitement brandished its pride and solidarity. All united, civil and military forces took part side by side in the rescue operations. Their uniforms were difficult to identify under the dust that covered them. Humanitarian organizations quickly deployed to coordinate actions and provide vital aid. Although hospitals were filled with the wounded, a military hospital was set up in record time, and doctors and nurses continued to work tirelessly to provide care.

Morocco buries its dead.

Sadly, almost 3,000 people lost their lives in this terrible cataclysm: teachers, imams, students who found themselves deprived of knowledge and learning from one day to the next. But, despite the tragedy that overwhelmed them, their courage never wavered. They worked together, collecting their books, slates and quills, creating improvised spaces to continue their lessons and learn the Koran, a custom that has been ingrained in the hearts of Moroccans for generations.

Children learning the Koran in a medersa.

Education, a national priority.

The Morocco of today has evolved considerably from its past, which was marked by a high rate of illiteracy. These days, education has become a national priority, and the greatest concern of all players at all levels of society is now the education of children. Whether being a parent in a big city like Casablanca or a remote village in the Atlas Mountains, the importance of education is universally recognised. This transformation is the result of a collective commitment to improving access to education.

Significant reforms have been undertaken, particularly for girls and children from rural or disadvantaged backgrounds. The Moroccan government has set up programmes to strengthen educational infrastructure, train competent teachers and modernise teaching methods. The country has gone from a situation of widespread illiteracy to a nation determined to invest in its human capital, which has become a central pillar of contemporary Moroccan society.

Amidst the rubble, *Aicha* stands, unable to comprehend what is happening. Her gaze fixed on the smoking ruins of her former home; she cannot stop calling all her missing children by their names. Her life has been turned upside down forever in a matter of seconds by the earthquake. Her family who were so important to her, her husband who had been her rock, her children who filled her home with joy had no chance of being found alive. They have gone far beyond, leaving behind them a heart filled with immeasurable pain.

Aicha is in a state of despair and is unable to overcome her difficult ordeal. She walks aimlessly through the ruins, trying to understand what has happened. She wonders if she'll ever be able to regain some sense of normalcy after learning of the immense loss she has just suffered. However, as she struggles to stand amidst the debris, a neighbor from the village climbs over the ruins with a plate of food in her hand, expressing her empathic support and offering her a shoulder to cry on and a hand to get up.

Aicha's life is not over, even if her loved ones are gone. She will never forget them, and she will continue to call them by their names, they will always live with her.

Mehdi, aged 13, contemplates the rubble of his ruined house, pondering the disaster that has just struck his village and his family. Clinging to a man in his seventies, *this latter*shares his own story of how he lost everything in the Agadir earthquake. He also tells *Mehdi* how he was able to rebuild his life, find new reasons to smile and regain hope, thanks to a community that helped him get over the hump. He explains to him that he has to pick himself up and learn to live again if he is to honor the memory of his family.

The after effects of the tragedy will never completely disappear; losing your whole family in a catastrophe is traumatic, and the extent of this feeling is still difficult to deal with. *Aicha* and *Mehdi*, like thousands of their fellow villagers, have lost not only all their loved ones, but also a large part of their identity, their daily routine and their emotional support. The words spoken will not soothe the pain they have suffered, but time will heal the wounds, and we hope they will find the strength to carry on.

No one can remain strong in front of death.

The testimony of a resident of Ouirgane, a village heavily impacted by its proximity to the epicenter, highlighted the lack of understanding of certain key issues. A man who has just lost his parents, his two sisters and several relatives and friends explains to a radio station host why the majority of people living in the disaster zones refuse to leave, despite the dangers. He says "It's not as simple as you might think; the deeper reality of this attachment can't be seen through city temperature glasses. The affectionate warmth of these houses at the ends of the earth, built deep in valleys or on mountaintops, is more than just global warming in the eyes of these villagers; it represents their identity and history, conjugued through the ages. They lived in a house handed down from generation to generation, and lived there with their grandparents, parents, uncles, cousins, brothers, and, and, and... Do you think it would be easy to forget everything and go somewhere else? No, they will not leave their homes until their loved ones have been found and burried. Then, once the rubble has been cleared, they will search for their personal belongings and household goods, if any remain, and rebuild their homes in the same place and in the same traditional way, if necessary. I confess i felt better nowhere than at my family's former home (emotional silence on air). Gathered with my family on the large esplanade of the house over a tagine and a cup of tea, staying awake until late at night contemplating the twinkling stars, it was the best moment of my life," he concludes tearfully.

The whole country was moved by the moving story of an elderly woman buried in the rubble of her home. Passers-by heard her cries for help and worked tirelessly to free her despite the risks. The tears she shed in gratitude and happiness were a powerful reminder of human strength and solidarity.

The spirit of solidarity: an elderly woman miraculously saved by volunteers.

"To those who love those who migrate to them. They find no envy in their hearts for what has been given to these immigrants. They prefer them to themselves, despite their poverty. Those who guard against their own greed are the blessed". Holy Quran 59: The Gathering.

According to some of the volunteers from the Gulf States, one of the things that caught their attention and that words cannot express was the ability of the stricken people to resist, while expressing their joy at seeing strangers again. *Ahmed*, an old man who had lost everything, his family and possessions, expressed his gratitude and insisted on offering them tea. Apart from his endurance in the face of tragedy, what surprised those most was the faith that remained in this nonagenarian of altruistic spirit, who never ceased to praise God that this destruction had affected villages and not towns. He affirmed that the opposite situation would have been far worse, and the villagers would not have had much to offer, just as they would not have been able to help their fellow city-dwellers in the same way as these latters do towards them.

Dozens of foreign tourists decided to extend their stay to help the victims. A highly commended action that was widely publicized via social networks.

One of the tourists present at the time told a foreign channel that what deeply moved him, beyond national cohesion, was the ten-year-old little girl who was looking for food amid the rubble to feed the cats following her. In such a tragic ordeal, in which this child has certainly lost at least one member of her family if she is not already an orphan, animals had a great place in her charitable soul.

Although donations follow adversity, any provisions collected to provide for the victims are but ephemeral objects. Nevertheless, support will remain firmly anchored in the minds of citizens deeply touched by the tragedy and, above all, by sharing and humanity.

The anonymous heroes who stood up in the darkness remind us that life is fragile and hangs on a very thin thread, and that Man can easily lose everything from one minute to the next, but kindness and compassion remain our strength to break through the darkest moments.

The man with the bicycle and the woman serving the soldiers.

As long as we continue to reach out to one another. As long as the earth that shook that night continues to support good-hearted people like the man on the bicycle, who wanted to do his bit, if only with half a sack of wheat. As long as the good lady who has only her dowry ring and gives it away as alms, or the brave woman who, in the midst of distress, forgets her losses and sorrows and prepares to eat for the soldiers, humanity will be fine and hope will remain.

The lords of the ring, wheat and the oil bottle. The bicycle of love. The blood donation queue. Yassine Bounou, child of the nation.

The people united in distress in the midst of tragedy. *Myriam*, a French-Moroccan doctor at the Paris hospitals, was another source of clarity in the darkness. After taking their leave with other colleagues, they left for Marrakech and arrived at the scene of the tragedy to help the injured. Their dedication has served as a model for this community, which is committed beyond its borders to helping its homeland.

Famous personalities who deeply cherish the country in which they live immediately mobilized to help the victims, like *Maitre Gims* who, following a concert in France, took the first available flight to join his family living just a few kilometers from the disaster zone. His appearance among the local associations to help them was a welcome moral reassurance before being a material support.

Maitre Gims comes to the aid of a village in chaos.

An emblematic figure in charity work also played an effective role in managing the disaster, thanks to his extensive international expertise. This was the case for former French minister and IMF Chairman *Dominique Strauss-Kahn*, who, as the head of the "Mekkil" association, stated, "Morocco is my second country. It has given me a lot, from Agadir where I spent my childhood, to Marra-kech where I live today. The Mekkil association, which I chair, has chosen the field of mother and child protection in the broadest sense of the term, in a modest attempt to give back to the Moroccans some of the benefits they have showered on me".

September 13, 2023. A duet on BFM from Marrakech, where Dominique Strauss Kahn currently resides.

British businessperson *Richard Branson*, head of the Virgin group and owner of numerous riads in the Al-Haouz region, immediately went to the scene to help the victims. The *Eve Branson* Foundation named after his mother, works to raise the standard of living for women and girls in the region.

The billionaire wrote on his twitter account, "Eve was an adventurer, writer, mother and compassionate friend to the women and girls of the High Atlas Mountains. A strong 6.8 magnitude earthquake has hit Morocco hard, we are working to activate a coordinated response to bring help where it is most needed and support recovery efforts. Our thoughts are with the Moroccan people.

Gad El Maleh, the beloved comedian, organized a show during which he raised almost five million dirhams for the victims of the earthquake. In the face of such altruistic acts, what can we say? Sometimes, silence is a blessing.

In a fascinating report broadcast on Medi1 TV, under the title "With Morocco from Washington", American journalist *Marc Faivli* quotesm, "In difficulty, we learn new lessons. We discover our friends and get facts we didn't know before".

Yassine Khaled, 13, is one of many children who were horrified by the scenes of the earthquake. He asked his mother's permission and launched an initiative, small in his eyes but very big in the eyes of Moroccans, to collect donations for the victims.

Yassine, who lives in the United States, says, "I was overwhelmed by a sense of relief when i decided to go and make a donation with my sister and mother. It's really sad what happened, and anything we can offer is very little.

Yassine and other children among the donations: USA.

At school, *Yassine* led a small army of friends and acquaintances in the hope that his urgent wish to collect as many donations as possible would come true, to ease the pain of the victims and fulfill his humanitarian and patriotic duty towards children like him who have lost everything. *Yassine* is a little hero and a mass of human feelings that have exploded across borders to write the epic of a people united despite distances, clinging to the values they have inherited from their parents, and passing them on to their children in a lasting way.

American actress and film producer *Ophray Winfery*, who adores Marrakech and describes it as a soul-filling place, expressed her solidarity by helping out with her own money.

Her compatriot *Maggy O'Neill*, visual artist, because of her great love of Morocco, has also dedicated part of her sales to benefiting the victims. She told Medi1 TV: "I've been to Morocco ten times in the last twelve years, and it's a special country for me for many reasons. As an artist, I know of no other place in the world that has influenced me in terms of creative spirit and handcrafted colors. The people there fill you with an unprecedented generosity, humanity and spirituality. If I could leave my job and go there to help in any way, I would do it tomorrow without hesitation".

Another News-look journalist named *Giorgio Cafiero* quotes, "Everyone is praying for Morocco these days".

Ophray Winfery *Maggy O'Neill.*

Why so much love, compassion and sympathy for a people who act spontaneously in favor of peace and respect for others? I think the answer lies in its authentic history, which springs from the depths of its soul, its blue skies, azure waters and high mountains, with the message of coexistence between nations.

"This is Morocco in the eyes of its lovers," concludes the American journalist.

It's not strange to see people come for a simple visit, then fall in love and wish to stay. Morocco, in addition to its sumptuous nature and pleasant climate, offers security, political stability and the infrastructure for a decent life.

Policy towards foreigners differs from country to cuntry, but in Morocco, despite differences in culture, origins or religious denominations, the population cohabits peacefully and everyone is considered a full citizen, not entirely apart. Tolerance remains a fundamental value of our society, which has always been a crossroads of cultures and civilizations. Moroccans are proud of their cultural and historical heritage, and are happy to share it. Tourism remains a vital sector of the country's economy, welcoming millions of visitors every year, which often places it in the top echelons of tourist destinations.

Although physical reconstruction is a considerable challenge, it is supported by hope and perseverance. The region will rise again, the streets will be filled with life, monuments will stand proud and smiles will replace the dust.

Over the course of time, the country has gone through prosperous and tumultuous times, but one constant remains: its unshakeable roots. The ups and downs of its history have forged the character of the nation. Successive generations have learned to face difficulties with courage, the trials and tribulations that have befallen the country have never succeeded in eroding its deep-rooted identity. Despite the pitfalls that stand like invisible ramparts around its borders, the country remains as indomitable as a sturdy oak in the midst of a storm. It resists the winds that try to uproot it, thanks to the ties that bind its people together. Strained relations with its eastern neighbour have often been a thorn in its side, but the country has never given in to the temptation of animosity. On the contrary, it has preferred to reach out and use diplomacy to ease conflicts and build bridges towards a more peaceful future.

Morocco has remained great not because of the size of its territory, but because of the grandeur of its soul. Its values, its culture and its history are all pillars on which it relies to remain strong. The challenges of the present only strengthen its determination to preserve its roots, and it continues to write history with its head held high.

Humanitarian aid from all over the world is accelerating, while the country is first trying to heal its wounds with its own resources. Nations came together to lend a helping hand, but Morocco was only able to enlist the help of four countries considered friends and allies: Spain, Great Britain, Qatar and the United Arab Emirates.

In the face of natural disasters, no country, whatever its size or economic weight, is immune to loss. However, every nation strives to limit damage and learn from adversity.Thoughtlessly requesting or accepting humanitarian aid is pointless and often leads to chaos and anarchy. In this respect, Morocco has taken a commendable decision to adopt a selective approach to foreign subsidies, as it is unethical to accept all international aid at random, to the detriment of other countries such as Libya, which is suffering more because of its devastating tragedy.

A military convoy distributing aid.

A country's decision to accept or refuse foreign humanitarian aid depends on a number of factors, such as its geographical location, the types of assistance required, diplomatic relations, domestic politics and its national capacity to cope with crises. It is possible that the acceptance of foreign aid poses problems of coordination in the management of the various humanitarian actors on the ground, or that diplomatic relations between a country providing aid and a country in need are influenced by external elements such as foreign policy, alliances or geopolitical tensions.

France in particular was not among the countries chosen for this humanitarian action. Instead, aid was channeled through associations, charities and volunteers, who courageously delivered it to the region. As a nation with a long tradition of friendship, the French and Moroccan peoples remain close friends. However, as a political state, and particularly under the presidency of *Emmanuel Macron*, diplomatic relations have unfortunately deteriorated and become more complex.

Morocco is a school that teaches its pupils the humanities, and the lesson the Master of the High Castle taught his disciples under the most difficult of circumstances was one of unprecedented spirituality. A lesson in ethics transformed into a compulsory exam worth taking note of. But the Moroccans, with all their dedication and professionalism, understood the task and answered the exam perfectly, with great skill. As assiduous students, they united behind their master, giving their blood, their time and their funds. What values that strongly deserve to be taught! Those, which give priority to the people first to exercise their duty before asking or accepting the help of a foreign master. His partial or total negative response, accompanied by his thanks for most of the proposals, was an unprecedented first, as no country faced with such an ordeal had ever refused help before. However, Morocco managed the situation rationally, addressing its children first with a coded message in the manner of Caesar, which the people understand very well: the lion, even when it falls, does not die as long as it is protected by its lioncubs.

During the earthquake, towns competed with each other for trucks to deliver aid, and all the humanitarian actions were visible in this dramatic scene. A hairdresser sets up his chair in the middle of the ruins and cuts the hair of the villagers to alleviate suffering and boost morale. An old man on a bicycle hands over half a sack of flour, perhaps all he owns, and rides away with his back bent. Doctors take their leave and rush to the aid of the wounded. A grieving woman invites her rescuers to eat and another removes her only ring. A group of Syrian restaurators living in Morocco rush to the scene and open a free mobile restaurant to serve the victims, seeing it as a minimum of duty to a country and a people who have welcomed them warmly. From the top of a ruined house, an old woman forgets her sorrows and makes her foreign guests laugh with endless anecdotes.

What mental strength and enviable faith!

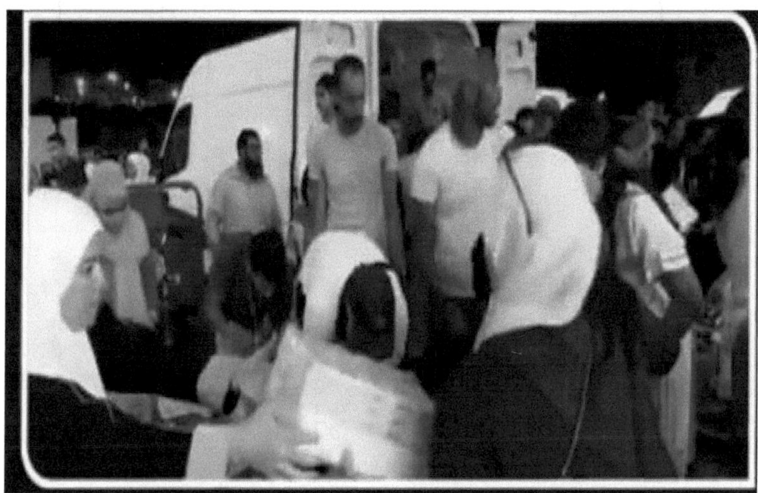

Donations speak to benefactors: "Enough!

The Moroccan is truly astonishing in his duality. He's quick to react to the most mundane things, from honking horns at rush hour to pointless quarrels in the streets or markets, but as soon as he perceives his community in danger or need, emotion takes over and he immediately rallies his forces to support his compatriots. This time, he sets off running, crawling or even leaning on crutches. A poignant example is that of the young disabled *Moulay Ali*, who didn't hesitate to contribute with a humble little bag of provisions. However, this bag contained much more than just food, it carried the quintessential message of love and solidarity that a human being can carry deep in his soul and be ready to offer to the whole of humanity.

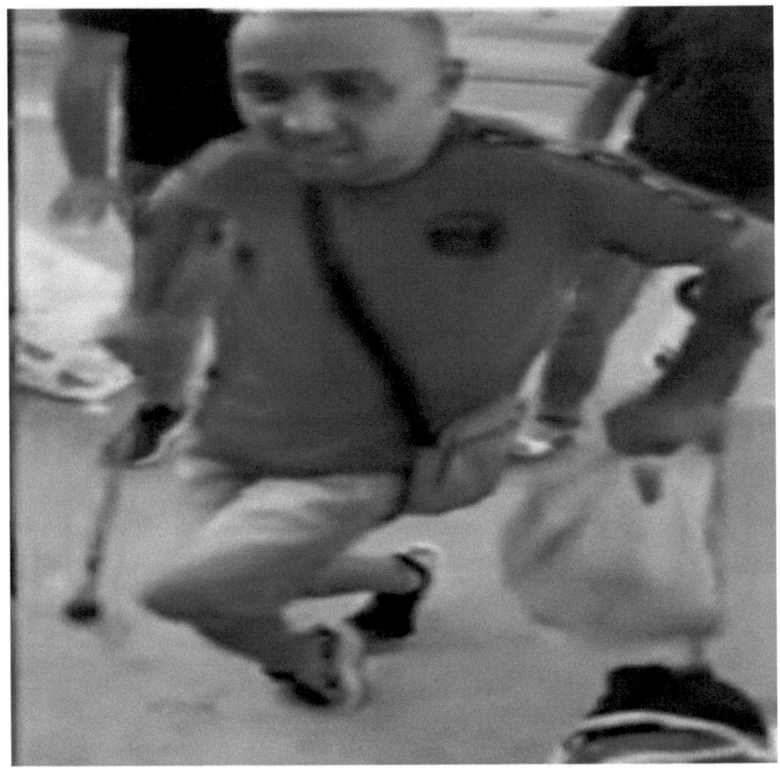

Thank you, Moulay Ali.

In this respect, one of the hidden reasons that most motivated the Moroccan national team in Qatar to give their all in the quarterfinal match was a deeply moving image broadcast by the coach in the dressing room during half time. This image captured an exceptional moment; a little disabled girl, sitting in a wheelchair, watching the previous match on a giant screen. When the national team won the match, the joy of this young fan was so intense that she almost fell out of her wheelchair leaping for joy. It was a poignant moment that touched the hearts of an entire nation. The image of this little girl had a profound impact on the team's players, reminding each of them of their moral duty on the pitch: not only to play for victory, but also to inspire and bring joy to supporters like this young girl. There were tears in the dressing room that day, as the players felt the responsibility and pride of representing their nation. This memorable image not only strengthened the resolve of the team, but also highlighted the power of sport to create moments of emotional connection between players, supporters and the nation as a whole.

These joyful and tragic events have revealed the hidden beauty and generosity that were buried in a hectic material life, and that only need a simple unclick to awaken them. And as we say so well in Arabic, "In Morocco, don't be surprised".

It's not strange to see someone leave their country and family just to look for work and be able to provide for their parents, siblings, children and even relatives. The importance of family is indisputable. Moroccans always support their loved ones in any way they can, and this deep connection reflects the ethical and moral human sensibility that reveals itself through acts of generosity and compassion innately passed down from father to son.

Military women, in addition to their professional duties in the army, played a crucial role in providing moral support to women and children in particular.

Thanks to her feminine nature, she was able to forge intimate emotional bonds with the victims, enabling a better understanding of their specific needs. She created a space dedicated to children, with lovingly attentive supervision, where they felt safe and in familial harmony.

Her presence created a more welcoming environment for women who had lost their families. Her compassion, guided by a heightened sensitivity and empathic understanding of emotional situations, put victims at ease and gave them the courage to express their grief and share their concerns. This emotional connection provided a psychological expertise that was more appeasing than the directive approach of her male colleagues.

Between women, we understand each other.

The movement of convoys from all the provinces of Morocco reminds us of those organized by our parents in 1975, when they loyally responded to the late King *Hassan II*'s call for a Green March and the liberation of the Moroccan Sahara. This latter was under Spanish occupation, and King *Hassan II* launched an historic appeal to his people to organise the Green March, a peaceful mobilisation aimed at recovering the occupied territories. Three hundred and fifty thousand Moroccans responded to this call, heading for the southern provinces with only flags to assert Morocco's sovereignty over these lands, and the Koran to anchor the teachings of the Holy Book in the region. Moroccans of all geographical, ethnic and social origins united in a single patriotic impulse. An overwhelming obedience, revealing the historical, cultural, religious and political ties that consolidated loyalty to the royal throne. The Green March has become a symbol of national unity and the strength of the Moroccan monarchy in the country's collective imagination.

The late King Hassan II's call to the Green March in 1975.

Today, Moroccans from southern provinces responded to the cries of their fellow citizens, expressing their full Moroccan identity and their deep attachment to the monarchy and territorial unity. Morocco is Sahara and the Sahara is Morocco.

The relationship between Morocco and Spain is complex and multifaceted, marked by historical, cultural, economic and political elements. Although territories such as the Sahara before, Ceuta and Melilla which are still claimed by Morocco, their relationship has aspects of cooperation and partnership. Spain is one of Morocco's main trading partners, and the two countries work together in various fields and maintain close economic relations.

In this respect, a major project is still in the pipeline, and people are waiting with hope to see it thruly one day. It concerns the idea of linking two continents via a bridge. This latter, often referred to as the "Strait Bridge or Gibraltar Bridge", would aim to establish a physical connection not only between two countries, but also between Europe and Africa, by crossing the Strait of Gibraltar.

The concept of this monumental bridge has been mooted for many years. Nevertheless, the realisation of such a project would be complex, requiring enormous financial resources, cutting-edge technical expertise and cooperation between nations. Considerable environmental and geopolitical challenges would have to be overcome.

If the project ever came to fruition, it would undoubtedly go down in the annals of history as one of most spectacular humankind construction projects.

Chapter 4
Determination and hope.

It is during difficult times that true capacity manifests itself. The Moroccan people did not lose their determination, but rather strengthened it, and their support was unconditional. Soccer fans have transformed themselves into an unbeatable army, fervently shouting "Go Morocco! For them, the challenge is more than just a ball that delights them or an earthquake that discourages them. It represents the very essence of nationhood, a symbol of resilience and pride.

The people have shown their will to overcome all obstacles in times of joy and sorrow. They have demonstrated their resilience, compassion and solidarity, whether on the soccer pitch in Qatar or in the rubble of Al-Haouz.

Every moment of Moroccan life is marked by tangible emotions, demonstrating that the soul of the country will remain solid as long as its children remain solidary, despite the difficulties of fate.

The Moroccan fan who committed his wallet to accompany his favorite team to Qatar, here he is, digging stones out of the mountains, and once again raising funds to help his victims. And as long as his love for his country remains undying, his strength will continue to be the pillar of the nation.

After difficulty comes ease. Although the tragedy that shook the region was devastating in its entirety, it also brought a ray of unexpected hope. The region's inhabitants, who had endured drought for decades, saw water miraculously emerge from the mountains. The new springs have had a comforting impact on life in the region, as they will generate interest in drinking and irrigating their land. Morale was boosted by this providence, demonstrating that nature can reserve surprises that bring welcome relief even after tragedy.

The soldier who moved an entire nation.

Interpretations of the catastrophes our planet has been experiencing of late resonate differently with everyone. Some see them in a purely scientific context, attributing them to natural forces. Others, on the other hand, seek to discuss human responsibility for these catastrophes, whether due to excessive industrial practices, underground activities, global warming or even evoking HAARP theories.

In an article in Figaro actualities, published by *Steve Tenré* on 17/05/2023 and updated on 16/09/2023, entitled: "Bombes sismiques, chemtrails, projet Haarp... Inside the secret of climate weapons".

He quotes: "The earthquake in Morocco and the floods in Libya have revived conspiracy theories about alleged weapons capable of triggering natural disasters. They are confronted with real climate modification projects. Was the earthquake in Morocco, which killed nearly 3,000 people, triggered by a "vibration bomb", as some Internet users claim? Are the floods in Libya, responsible for thousands of deaths, the work of a "rain machine"? What about the recent wildfires in Hawaii, where hundreds of people disappeared, allegedly triggered by an "energy weapon", according to multiple publications on social networks?

In recent years, this type of accusation has been made with every natural disaster," he concludes.

However, despite the many rumors and varied interpretations and speculations, and despite the abundance of soothsayers, sorcerers and charlatans, the country remains secure in the knowledge that nothing will trouble it or jeopardize its existence, as long as its citizens remain guided by their attachment to their values, and above all united and aligned behind an enlightened and rational sovereign.

Thanks to its glorious past and dynamic present, Morocco continues to inspire and amaze those who have the opportunity to discover its hidden treasures. Its history is a powerful reminder of the richness that can emerge from a nation's diversity and resilience. It has repeatedly demonstrated its soft power as a united and supportive nation. It was at the pinnacle of civic mindedness and responsibility, rallying to support its heroes in easy times, and to wipe the dust off the foreheads of its stricken fellow citizens, relentlessly expressing its determination to face difficulties head on.

The country and its people now look to the future with an unshakeable determination to write its lines in radiant ink, whether of success or defeat, joy or sorrow. They work together to overcome challenges, build a better tomorrow and mark a history filled with emotion, challenge and solidarity.

As I come to the end of this story, after having traversed the moments of joy, sorrow and adventure experienced by a people novelist from a local novel, a feeling of pride overwhelms me, as I hope to have covered it in a sufficiently concise manner.

At this very moment, His Majesty the King has just officially announced Morocco's participation in the organization of the 2030 World Cup. I can't let this extraordinary news go unmentioned, as it sheds light on the tragic chapter of Al-Haouz. Morocco will be hosting a major international event in addition to the African Cup of Nations in 2025, a welcome development that reflects the country's considerable efforts. It would be hard not to be excited by this announcement. Once again, the people will embark on a new race in the trail to promote their country and forget the earthquake and the pain that came from its bowels. It will also be preparing to shine on the international stage by hosting these two prestigious forums, which will be an opportunity to raise its profile once again and demonstrate its essential role in representing its country. The twelfth player on the Qatar and Al-Haouz pitch will stand proudly in support of his national team once again. The stadiums will resound with patriotic chants and the crowds will astonish the public when they passionately sing their sacred flag.

The long awaited World Cup will be a historic moment for Morocco and for the African continent. The country has a successful track record in hosting such sporting events, having staged smaller tournaments such as the FIFA World Cup in 2010, and is ready to rise to the challenge once again. Modern pitches and first-class infrastructure will be on hand to welcome the participating teams and fans from all over the world. Morocco's passion for soccer will be palpable in the stadiums, where the festive atmosphere will create unforgettable memories for visitors. By organizing this major sporting event, Morocco aims to promote fair play, cultural diversity and world unity. It will also be displaying its expertise and success in fields such as tourism, industry and information technology.

These two events are much more than just sporting competitions, they are a showcase for the country's dynamism and efforts to ensure sustainable development, a platform for dialogue between nations and a link where borders disappear and cultures mingle. In addition to the economic spin-offs and tourist appeal, they help to strengthen national pride.

With such a major organization, our people will have the opportunity to showcase their history and identity more than ever, and demonstrate their ability to welcome others through their hospitality and the richness of their cultural and culinary traditions in particular. It also confirms its role as a leader in Africa and its desire to contribute to the continent's influence.

The upcoming dates of Africa 2025 and the World 2030 will be promising, and the nation will see many major worksites and projects in the run-up to these dates, adding to its determination to grow and prosper further. The kingdom of challenges will shine brightly, reminding us of its greatness and generosity, and the people will be ready to open their doors to the world.

Morocco has known moments of joy and sorrow, but difficult times will never deter it. The country and its people are one body, and if one organ complains, the whole body suffers from insomnia and fever. It will continue to be characterized by the development of its capacities and its economic and cultural potential, it will continue to promote its heritage and knowledge on an international scale, and it will do so thanks to the common will between a wise King and a predominantly young and dynamic people.

"God, the fatherland, the King".

O earth!

In the setting of your majestic mountains, you reveal precious wonders.

Under the sun and the joyful rains, your splendor awakens sleeping eras.

In the joy that delights my blessed heart, I acclaim your slogan and glorious times.

In joy, my passionate heart, celebrates your history that shaped it.

Childhood laughter, songs and stories, filled me with joy, O local novel!

And when the shadow of torment darkens my days, I remain upright and hopeful forever.

That despite the adversity ahead, I remain confident with hope.

Conditional times teach us wisely, that your unconditional love will live forever.

In the whirlpools of your waves we learn, that in joy and sorrow we follow you.

In joy, in sorrow and in my soul, your name shines in me like a flame.

In joy, in sorrow I am sincere, you are cherished by my flesh, oh earth my dear!

Med Labane.

May you live forever.

Printed by Books on Demand GmbH, Norderstedt / Germany